My Book of
Finances
and
Expenses

Monthly Bill Organizer
Notebook

@ Journals & Notebooks

@ Journals & Notebooks

Food	Gadgets	Other Expenses

Insurance	Payment	Date Paid

Utilities	Payment	Date Paid
Electricity		
Water		
Sanitation		
Phone service		
Internet service		
Cable TV		
Gas		
Total =		

Date	Bill	Amount	Jan	Feb	Mar	Apr	May	Jun	Jul	Aug	Sep	Oct	Nov	Dec

Monthly Income:　　Extra Income:　　Total Income:　　Total Paid Out:　　Cash Available:

Food	Gadgets	Other Expenses

Insurance	Payment	Date Paid

Utilities	Payment	Date Paid
Electricity		
Water		
Sanitation		
Phone service		
Internet service		
Cable TV		
Gas		
Total =		

Date	Bill	Amount	Jan	Feb	Mar	Apr	May	Jun	Jul	Aug	Sep	Oct	Nov	Dec

Monthly Income: Extra Income: Total Income: Total Paid Out: Cash Available:

Food	Gadgets	Other Expenses

Insurance	Payment	Date Paid

Utilities	Payment	Date Paid
Electricity		
Water		
Sanitation		
Phone service		
Internet service		
Cable TV		
Gas		
Total =		

Date	Bill	Amount	Jan	Feb	Mar	Apr	May	Jun	Jul	Aug	Sep	Oct	Nov	Dec

Monthly Income: Extra Income: Total Income: Total Paid Out: Cash Available:

Food	Gadgets	Other Expenses

Insurance	Payment	Date Paid

Utilities	Payment	Date Paid
Electricity		
Water		
Sanitation		
Phone service		
Internet service		
Cable TV		
Gas		
Total =		

Date	Bill	Amount	Jan	Feb	Mar	Apr	May	Jun	Jul	Aug	Sep	Oct	Nov	Dec

Monthly Income: Extra Income: Total Income: Total Paid Out: Cash Available:

Food	Gadgets	Other Expenses

Insurance	Payment	Date Paid

Utilities	Payment	Date Paid
Electricity		
Water		
Sanitation		
Phone service		
Internet service		
Cable TV		
Gas		
Total =		

Date	Bill	Amount	Jan	Feb	Mar	Apr	May	Jun	Jul	Aug	Sep	Oct	Nov	Dec

Monthly Income: Extra Income: Total Income: Total Paid Out: Cash Available:

Food	Gadgets	Other Expenses

Insurance	Payment	Date Paid

Utilities	Payment	Date Paid
Electricity		
Water		
Sanitation		
Phone service		
Internet service		
Cable TV		
Gas		
Total =		

Date	Bill	Amount	Jan	Feb	Mar	Apr	May	Jun	Jul	Aug	Sep	Oct	Nov	Dec

Monthly Income: Extra Income: Total Income: Total Paid Out: Cash Available:

Food	Gadgets	Other Expenses

Insurance	Payment	Date Paid

Utilities	Payment	Date Paid
Electricity		
Water		
Sanitation		
Phone service		
Internet service		
Cable TV		
Gas		
Total =		

Date	Bill	Amount	Jan	Feb	Mar	Apr	May	Jun	Jul	Aug	Sep	Oct	Nov	Dec

Monthly Income: Extra Income: Total Income: Total Paid Out: Cash Available:

Food	Gadgets	Other Expenses

Insurance	Payment	Date Paid

Utilities	Payment	Date Paid
Electricity		
Water		
Sanitation		
Phone service		
Internet service		
Cable TV		
Gas		
Total =		

Date	Bill	Amount	Jan	Feb	Mar	Apr	May	Jun	Jul	Aug	Sep	Oct	Nov	Dec

Monthly Income: Extra Income: Total Income: Total Paid Out: Cash Available:

Food	Gadgets	Other Expenses

Insurance	Payment	Date Paid

Utilities	Payment	Date Paid
Electricity		
Water		
Sanitation		
Phone service		
Internet service		
Cable TV		
Gas		
Total =		

Date	Bill	Amount	Jan	Feb	Mar	Apr	May	Jun	Jul	Aug	Sep	Oct	Nov	Dec

Monthly Income: Extra Income: Total Income: Total Paid Out: Cash Available:

Food	Gadgets	Other Expenses

Insurance	Payment	Date Paid

Utilities	Payment	Date Paid
Electricity		
Water		
Sanitation		
Phone service		
Internet service		
Cable TV		
Gas		
Total =		

Date	Bill	Amount	Jan	Feb	Mar	Apr	May	Jun	Jul	Aug	Sep	Oct	Nov	Dec

Monthly Income: Extra Income: Total Income: Total Paid Out: Cash Available:

Food	Gadgets	Other Expenses

Insurance	Payment	Date Paid

Utilities	Payment	Date Paid
Electricity		
Water		
Sanitation		
Phone service		
Internet service		
Cable TV		
Gas		
Total =		

Date	Bill	Amount	Jan	Feb	Mar	Apr	May	Jun	Jul	Aug	Sep	Oct	Nov	Dec
			☐	☐	☐	☐	☐	☐	☐	☐	☐	☐	☐	☐
			☐	☐	☐	☐	☐	☐	☐	☐	☐	☐	☐	☐
			☐	☐	☐	☐	☐	☐	☐	☐	☐	☐	☐	☐
			☐	☐	☐	☐	☐	☐	☐	☐	☐	☐	☐	☐
			☐	☐	☐	☐	☐	☐	☐	☐	☐	☐	☐	☐
			☐	☐	☐	☐	☐	☐	☐	☐	☐	☐	☐	☐
			☐	☐	☐	☐	☐	☐	☐	☐	☐	☐	☐	☐
			☐	☐	☐	☐	☐	☐	☐	☐	☐	☐	☐	☐
			☐	☐	☐	☐	☐	☐	☐	☐	☐	☐	☐	☐
			☐	☐	☐	☐	☐	☐	☐	☐	☐	☐	☐	☐
			☐	☐	☐	☐	☐	☐	☐	☐	☐	☐	☐	☐
			☐	☐	☐	☐	☐	☐	☐	☐	☐	☐	☐	☐
			☐	☐	☐	☐	☐	☐	☐	☐	☐	☐	☐	☐

Monthly Income: Extra Income: Total Income: Total Paid Out: Cash Available:

Food	Gadgets	Other Expenses

Insurance	Payment	Date Paid

Utilities	Payment	Date Paid
Electricity		
Water		
Sanitation		
Phone service		
Internet service		
Cable TV		
Gas		
Total =		

Date	Bill	Amount	Jan	Feb	Mar	Apr	May	Jun	Jul	Aug	Sep	Oct	Nov	Dec
			☐	☐	☐	☐	☐	☐	☐	☐	☐	☐	☐	☐
			☐	☐	☐	☐	☐	☐	☐	☐	☐	☐	☐	☐
			☐	☐	☐	☐	☐	☐	☐	☐	☐	☐	☐	☐
			☐	☐	☐	☐	☐	☐	☐	☐	☐	☐	☐	☐
			☐	☐	☐	☐	☐	☐	☐	☐	☐	☐	☐	☐
			☐	☐	☐	☐	☐	☐	☐	☐	☐	☐	☐	☐
			☐	☐	☐	☐	☐	☐	☐	☐	☐	☐	☐	☐
			☐	☐	☐	☐	☐	☐	☐	☐	☐	☐	☐	☐
			☐	☐	☐	☐	☐	☐	☐	☐	☐	☐	☐	☐
			☐	☐	☐	☐	☐	☐	☐	☐	☐	☐	☐	☐
			☐	☐	☐	☐	☐	☐	☐	☐	☐	☐	☐	☐
			☐	☐	☐	☐	☐	☐	☐	☐	☐	☐	☐	☐
			☐	☐	☐	☐	☐	☐	☐	☐	☐	☐	☐	☐
			☐	☐	☐	☐	☐	☐	☐	☐	☐	☐	☐	☐

Monthly Income: Extra Income: Total Income: Total Paid Out: Cash Available:

Food	Gadgets	Other Expenses

Insurance	Payment	Date Paid

Utilities	Payment	Date Paid
Electricity		
Water		
Sanitation		
Phone service		
Internet service		
Cable TV		
Gas		
Total =		

Date	Bill	Amount	Jan	Feb	Mar	Apr	May	Jun	Jul	Aug	Sep	Oct	Nov	Dec

Monthly Income: Extra Income: Total Income: Total Paid Out: Cash Available:

Food	Gadgets	Other Expenses

Insurance	Payment	Date Paid

Utilities	Payment	Date Paid
Electricity		
Water		
Sanitation		
Phone service		
Internet service		
Cable TV		
Gas		
Total =		

Date	Bill	Amount	Jan	Feb	Mar	Apr	May	Jun	Jul	Aug	Sep	Oct	Nov	Dec

Monthly Income: Extra Income: Total Income: Total Paid Out: Cash Available:

Food	Gadgets	Other Expenses

Insurance	Payment	Date Paid

Utilities	Payment	Date Paid
Electricity		
Water		
Sanitation		
Phone service		
Internet service		
Cable TV		
Gas		
Total =		

Date	Bill	Amount	Jan	Feb	Mar	Apr	May	Jun	Jul	Aug	Sep	Oct	Nov	Dec

Monthly Income: Extra Income: Total Income: Total Paid Out: Cash Available:

Food	Gadgets	Other Expenses

Insurance	Payment	Date Paid

Utilities	Payment	Date Paid
Electricity		
Water		
Sanitation		
Phone service		
Internet service		
Cable TV		
Gas		
Total =		

Date	Bill	Amount	Jan	Feb	Mar	Apr	May	Jun	Jul	Aug	Sep	Oct	Nov	Dec
			☐	☐	☐	☐	☐	☐	☐	☐	☐	☐	☐	☐
			☐	☐	☐	☐	☐	☐	☐	☐	☐	☐	☐	☐
			☐	☐	☐	☐	☐	☐	☐	☐	☐	☐	☐	☐
			☐	☐	☐	☐	☐	☐	☐	☐	☐	☐	☐	☐
			☐	☐	☐	☐	☐	☐	☐	☐	☐	☐	☐	☐
			☐	☐	☐	☐	☐	☐	☐	☐	☐	☐	☐	☐
			☐	☐	☐	☐	☐	☐	☐	☐	☐	☐	☐	☐
			☐	☐	☐	☐	☐	☐	☐	☐	☐	☐	☐	☐
			☐	☐	☐	☐	☐	☐	☐	☐	☐	☐	☐	☐
			☐	☐	☐	☐	☐	☐	☐	☐	☐	☐	☐	☐
			☐	☐	☐	☐	☐	☐	☐	☐	☐	☐	☐	☐
			☐	☐	☐	☐	☐	☐	☐	☐	☐	☐	☐	☐
			☐	☐	☐	☐	☐	☐	☐	☐	☐	☐	☐	☐

Monthly Income: Extra Income: Total Income: Total Paid Out: Cash Available:

Food	Gadgets	Other Expenses

Insurance	Payment	Date Paid

Utilities	Payment	Date Paid
Electricity		
Water		
Sanitation		
Phone service		
Internet service		
Cable TV		
Gas		
Total =		

Date	Bill	Amount	Jan	Feb	Mar	Apr	May	Jun	Jul	Aug	Sep	Oct	Nov	Dec

Monthly Income: Extra Income: Total Income: Total Paid Out: Cash Available:

Food	Gadgets	Other Expenses

Insurance	Payment	Date Paid

Utilities	Payment	Date Paid
Electricity		
Water		
Sanitation		
Phone service		
Internet service		
Cable TV		
Gas		
Total =		

Date	Bill	Amount	Jan	Feb	Mar	Apr	May	Jun	Jul	Aug	Sep	Oct	Nov	Dec

Monthly Income: Extra Income: Total Income: Total Paid Out: Cash Available:

Food	Gadgets	Other Expenses

Insurance	Payment	Date Paid

Utilities	Payment	Date Paid
Electricity		
Water		
Sanitation		
Phone service		
Internet service		
Cable TV		
Gas		
Total =		

Date	Bill	Amount	Jan	Feb	Mar	Apr	May	Jun	Jul	Aug	Sep	Oct	Nov	Dec

Monthly Income: Extra Income: Total Income: Total Paid Out: Cash Available:

Food	Gadgets	Other Expenses

Insurance	Payment	Date Paid

Utilities	Payment	Date Paid
Electricity		
Water		
Sanitation		
Phone service		
Internet service		
Cable TV		
Gas		
Total =		

Date	Bill	Amount	Jan	Feb	Mar	Apr	May	Jun	Jul	Aug	Sep	Oct	Nov	Dec

Monthly Income: Extra Income: Total Income: Total Paid Out: Cash Available:

Food	Gadgets	Other Expenses

Insurance	Payment	Date Paid

Utilities	Payment	Date Paid
Electricity		
Water		
Sanitation		
Phone service		
Internet service		
Cable TV		
Gas		
Total =		

Date	Bill	Amount	Jan	Feb	Mar	Apr	May	Jun	Jul	Aug	Sep	Oct	Nov	Dec

Monthly Income: Extra Income: Total Income: Total Paid Out: Cash Available:

Food	Gadgets	Other Expenses

Insurance	Payment	Date Paid

Utilities	Payment	Date Paid
Electricity		
Water		
Sanitation		
Phone service		
Internet service		
Cable TV		
Gas		
Total =		

Date	Bill	Amount	Jan	Feb	Mar	Apr	May	Jun	Jul	Aug	Sep	Oct	Nov	Dec

Monthly Income: Extra Income: Total Income: Total Paid Out: Cash Available:

Food	Gadgets	Other Expenses

Insurance	Payment	Date Paid

Utilities	Payment	Date Paid
Electricity		
Water		
Sanitation		
Phone service		
Internet service		
Cable TV		
Gas		
Total =		

Date	Bill	Amount	Jan	Feb	Mar	Apr	May	Jun	Jul	Aug	Sep	Oct	Nov	Dec

Monthly Income: Extra Income: Total Income: Total Paid Out: Cash Available:

Food	Gadgets	Other Expenses

Insurance	Payment	Date Paid

Utilities	Payment	Date Paid
Electricity		
Water		
Sanitation		
Phone service		
Internet service		
Cable TV		
Gas		
Total =		

Date	Bill	Amount	Jan	Feb	Mar	Apr	May	Jun	Jul	Aug	Sep	Oct	Nov	Dec
			☐	☐	☐	☐	☐	☐	☐	☐	☐	☐	☐	☐
			☐	☐	☐	☐	☐	☐	☐	☐	☐	☐	☐	☐
			☐	☐	☐	☐	☐	☐	☐	☐	☐	☐	☐	☐
			☐	☐	☐	☐	☐	☐	☐	☐	☐	☐	☐	☐
			☐	☐	☐	☐	☐	☐	☐	☐	☐	☐	☐	☐
			☐	☐	☐	☐	☐	☐	☐	☐	☐	☐	☐	☐
			☐	☐	☐	☐	☐	☐	☐	☐	☐	☐	☐	☐
			☐	☐	☐	☐	☐	☐	☐	☐	☐	☐	☐	☐
			☐	☐	☐	☐	☐	☐	☐	☐	☐	☐	☐	☐
			☐	☐	☐	☐	☐	☐	☐	☐	☐	☐	☐	☐
			☐	☐	☐	☐	☐	☐	☐	☐	☐	☐	☐	☐
			☐	☐	☐	☐	☐	☐	☐	☐	☐	☐	☐	☐
			☐	☐	☐	☐	☐	☐	☐	☐	☐	☐	☐	☐

Monthly Income: Extra Income: Total Income: Total Paid Out: Cash Available:

Food	Gadgets	Other Expenses

Insurance	Payment	Date Paid

Utilities	Payment	Date Paid
Electricity		
Water		
Sanitation		
Phone service		
Internet service		
Cable TV		
Gas		
Total =		

Date	Bill	Amount	Jan	Feb	Mar	Apr	May	Jun	Jul	Aug	Sep	Oct	Nov	Dec

Monthly Income: Extra Income: Total Income: Total Paid Out: Cash Available:

Food	Gadgets	Other Expenses

Insurance	Payment	Date Paid

Utilities	Payment	Date Paid
Electricity		
Water		
Sanitation		
Phone service		
Internet service		
Cable TV		
Gas		
Total =		

Date	Bill	Amount	Jan	Feb	Mar	Apr	May	Jun	Jul	Aug	Sep	Oct	Nov	Dec

Monthly Income:　　Extra Income:　　Total Income:　　Total Paid Out:　Cash Available:

Food	Gadgets	Other Expenses

Insurance	Payment	Date Paid

Utilities	Payment	Date Paid
Electricity		
Water		
Sanitation		
Phone service		
Internet service		
Cable TV		
Gas		
Total =		

Date	Bill	Amount	Jan	Feb	Mar	Apr	May	Jun	Jul	Aug	Sep	Oct	Nov	Dec

Monthly Income: Extra Income: Total Income: Total Paid Out: Cash Available:

Food	Gadgets	Other Expenses

Insurance	Payment	Date Paid

Utilities	Payment	Date Paid
Electricity		
Water		
Sanitation		
Phone service		
Internet service		
Cable TV		
Gas		
Total =		

Date	Bill	Amount	Jan	Feb	Mar	Apr	May	Jun	Jul	Aug	Sep	Oct	Nov	Dec

Monthly Income: Extra Income: Total Income: Total Paid Out: Cash Available:

Food	Gadgets	Other Expenses

Insurance	Payment	Date Paid

Utilities	Payment	Date Paid
Electricity		
Water		
Sanitation		
Phone service		
Internet service		
Cable TV		
Gas		
Total =		

Date	Bill	Amount	Jan	Feb	Mar	Apr	May	Jun	Jul	Aug	Sep	Oct	Nov	Dec
			☐	☐	☐	☐	☐	☐	☐	☐	☐	☐	☐	☐
			☐	☐	☐	☐	☐	☐	☐	☐	☐	☐	☐	☐
			☐	☐	☐	☐	☐	☐	☐	☐	☐	☐	☐	☐
			☐	☐	☐	☐	☐	☐	☐	☐	☐	☐	☐	☐
			☐	☐	☐	☐	☐	☐	☐	☐	☐	☐	☐	☐
			☐	☐	☐	☐	☐	☐	☐	☐	☐	☐	☐	☐
			☐	☐	☐	☐	☐	☐	☐	☐	☐	☐	☐	☐
			☐	☐	☐	☐	☐	☐	☐	☐	☐	☐	☐	☐
			☐	☐	☐	☐	☐	☐	☐	☐	☐	☐	☐	☐
			☐	☐	☐	☐	☐	☐	☐	☐	☐	☐	☐	☐
			☐	☐	☐	☐	☐	☐	☐	☐	☐	☐	☐	☐
			☐	☐	☐	☐	☐	☐	☐	☐	☐	☐	☐	☐
			☐	☐	☐	☐	☐	☐	☐	☐	☐	☐	☐	☐
			☐	☐	☐	☐	☐	☐	☐	☐	☐	☐	☐	☐

Monthly Income: Extra Income: Total Income: Total Paid Out: Cash Available:

Food	Gadgets	Other Expenses

Insurance	Payment	Date Paid

Utilities	Payment	Date Paid
Electricity		
Water		
Sanitation		
Phone service		
Internet service		
Cable TV		
Gas		
Total =		

Date	Bill	Amount	Jan	Feb	Mar	Apr	May	Jun	Jul	Aug	Sep	Oct	Nov	Dec
			☐	☐	☐	☐	☐	☐	☐	☐	☐	☐	☐	☐
			☐	☐	☐	☐	☐	☐	☐	☐	☐	☐	☐	☐
			☐	☐	☐	☐	☐	☐	☐	☐	☐	☐	☐	☐
			☐	☐	☐	☐	☐	☐	☐	☐	☐	☐	☐	☐
			☐	☐	☐	☐	☐	☐	☐	☐	☐	☐	☐	☐
			☐	☐	☐	☐	☐	☐	☐	☐	☐	☐	☐	☐
			☐	☐	☐	☐	☐	☐	☐	☐	☐	☐	☐	☐
			☐	☐	☐	☐	☐	☐	☐	☐	☐	☐	☐	☐
			☐	☐	☐	☐	☐	☐	☐	☐	☐	☐	☐	☐
			☐	☐	☐	☐	☐	☐	☐	☐	☐	☐	☐	☐
			☐	☐	☐	☐	☐	☐	☐	☐	☐	☐	☐	☐
			☐	☐	☐	☐	☐	☐	☐	☐	☐	☐	☐	☐
			☐	☐	☐	☐	☐	☐	☐	☐	☐	☐	☐	☐

Monthly Income: Extra Income: Total Income: Total Paid Out: Cash Available:

Food	Gadgets	Other Expenses

Insurance	Payment	Date Paid

Utilities	Payment	Date Paid
Electricity		
Water		
Sanitation		
Phone service		
Internet service		
Cable TV		
Gas		
Total =		

Date	Bill	Amount	Jan	Feb	Mar	Apr	May	Jun	Jul	Aug	Sep	Oct	Nov	Dec

Monthly Income: Extra Income: Total Income: Total Paid Out: Cash Available:

Food	Gadgets	Other Expenses

Insurance	Payment	Date Paid

Utilities	Payment	Date Paid
Electricity		
Water		
Sanitation		
Phone service		
Internet service		
Cable TV		
Gas		
Total =		

Date	Bill	Amount	Jan	Feb	Mar	Apr	May	Jun	Jul	Aug	Sep	Oct	Nov	Dec

Monthly Income: Extra Income: Total Income: Total Paid Out: Cash Available:

Food	Gadgets	Other Expenses

Insurance	Payment	Date Paid

Utilities	Payment	Date Paid
Electricity		
Water		
Sanitation		
Phone service		
Internet service		
Cable TV		
Gas		
Total =		

Date	Bill	Amount	Jan	Feb	Mar	Apr	May	Jun	Jul	Aug	Sep	Oct	Nov	Dec
_____	_____	_____	☐	☐	☐	☐	☐	☐	☐	☐	☐	☐	☐	☐
_____	_____	_____	☐	☐	☐	☐	☐	☐	☐	☐	☐	☐	☐	☐
_____	_____	_____	☐	☐	☐	☐	☐	☐	☐	☐	☐	☐	☐	☐
_____	_____	_____	☐	☐	☐	☐	☐	☐	☐	☐	☐	☐	☐	☐
_____	_____	_____	☐	☐	☐	☐	☐	☐	☐	☐	☐	☐	☐	☐
_____	_____	_____	☐	☐	☐	☐	☐	☐	☐	☐	☐	☐	☐	☐
_____	_____	_____	☐	☐	☐	☐	☐	☐	☐	☐	☐	☐	☐	☐
_____	_____	_____	☐	☐	☐	☐	☐	☐	☐	☐	☐	☐	☐	☐
_____	_____	_____	☐	☐	☐	☐	☐	☐	☐	☐	☐	☐	☐	☐
_____	_____	_____	☐	☐	☐	☐	☐	☐	☐	☐	☐	☐	☐	☐
_____	_____	_____	☐	☐	☐	☐	☐	☐	☐	☐	☐	☐	☐	☐
_____	_____	_____	☐	☐	☐	☐	☐	☐	☐	☐	☐	☐	☐	☐
_____	_____	_____	☐	☐	☐	☐	☐	☐	☐	☐	☐	☐	☐	☐
_____	_____	_____	☐	☐	☐	☐	☐	☐	☐	☐	☐	☐	☐	☐

Monthly Income: Extra Income: Total Income: Total Paid Out: Cash Available:

Food	Gadgets	Other Expenses

Insurance	Payment	Date Paid

Utilities	Payment	Date Paid
Electricity		
Water		
Sanitation		
Phone service		
Internet service		
Cable TV		
Gas		
Total =		

Date	Bill	Amount	Jan	Feb	Mar	Apr	May	Jun	Jul	Aug	Sep	Oct	Nov	Dec

Monthly Income: Extra Income: Total Income: Total Paid Out: Cash Available:

Food	Gadgets	Other Expenses

Insurance	Payment	Date Paid

Utilities	Payment	Date Paid
Electricity		
Water		
Sanitation		
Phone service		
Internet service		
Cable TV		
Gas		
Total =		

Date	Bill	Amount	Jan	Feb	Mar	Apr	May	Jun	Jul	Aug	Sep	Oct	Nov	Dec

Monthly Income: Extra Income: Total Income: Total Paid Out: Cash Available:

Food	Gadgets	Other Expenses

Insurance	Payment	Date Paid

Utilities	Payment	Date Paid
Electricity		
Water		
Sanitation		
Phone service		
Internet service		
Cable TV		
Gas		
Total =		

Date	Bill	Amount	Jan	Feb	Mar	Apr	May	Jun	Jul	Aug	Sep	Oct	Nov	Dec

Monthly Income: Extra Income: Total Income: Total Paid Out: Cash Available:

Food	Gadgets	Other Expenses

Insurance	Payment	Date Paid

Utilities	Payment	Date Paid
Electricity		
Water		
Sanitation		
Phone service		
Internet service		
Cable TV		
Gas		
Total =		

Date	Bill	Amount	Jan	Feb	Mar	Apr	May	Jun	Jul	Aug	Sep	Oct	Nov	Dec
___	___	___	☐	☐	☐	☐	☐	☐	☐	☐	☐	☐	☐	☐
___	___	___	☐	☐	☐	☐	☐	☐	☐	☐	☐	☐	☐	☐
___	___	___	☐	☐	☐	☐	☐	☐	☐	☐	☐	☐	☐	☐
___	___	___	☐	☐	☐	☐	☐	☐	☐	☐	☐	☐	☐	☐
___	___	___	☐	☐	☐	☐	☐	☐	☐	☐	☐	☐	☐	☐
___	___	___	☐	☐	☐	☐	☐	☐	☐	☐	☐	☐	☐	☐
___	___	___	☐	☐	☐	☐	☐	☐	☐	☐	☐	☐	☐	☐
___	___	___	☐	☐	☐	☐	☐	☐	☐	☐	☐	☐	☐	☐
___	___	___	☐	☐	☐	☐	☐	☐	☐	☐	☐	☐	☐	☐
___	___	___	☐	☐	☐	☐	☐	☐	☐	☐	☐	☐	☐	☐
___	___	___	☐	☐	☐	☐	☐	☐	☐	☐	☐	☐	☐	☐
___	___	___	☐	☐	☐	☐	☐	☐	☐	☐	☐	☐	☐	☐
___	___	___	☐	☐	☐	☐	☐	☐	☐	☐	☐	☐	☐	☐
___	___	___	☐	☐	☐	☐	☐	☐	☐	☐	☐	☐	☐	☐

Monthly Income: Extra Income: Total Income: Total Paid Out: Cash Available:

Food	Gadgets	Other Expenses

Insurance	Payment	Date Paid

Utilities	Payment	Date Paid
Electricity		
Water		
Sanitation		
Phone service		
Internet service		
Cable TV		
Gas		
Total =		

Date	Bill	Amount	Jan	Feb	Mar	Apr	May	Jun	Jul	Aug	Sep	Oct	Nov	Dec

Monthly Income: Extra Income: Total Income: Total Paid Out: Cash Available:

Food	Gadgets	Other Expenses

Insurance	Payment	Date Paid

Utilities	Payment	Date Paid
Electricity		
Water		
Sanitation		
Phone service		
Internet service		
Cable TV		
Gas		
Total =		

Date	Bill	Amount	Jan	Feb	Mar	Apr	May	Jun	Jul	Aug	Sep	Oct	Nov	Dec

Monthly Income: Extra Income: Total Income: Total Paid Out: Cash Available:

Food	Gadgets	Other Expenses

Insurance	Payment	Date Paid

Utilities	Payment	Date Paid
Electricity		
Water		
Sanitation		
Phone service		
Internet service		
Cable TV		
Gas		
Total =		

Date	Bill	Amount	Jan	Feb	Mar	Apr	May	Jun	Jul	Aug	Sep	Oct	Nov	Dec

Monthly Income: Extra Income: Total Income: Total Paid Out: Cash Available:

Food	Gadgets	Other Expenses

Insurance	Payment	Date Paid

Utilities	Payment	Date Paid
Electricity		
Water		
Sanitation		
Phone service		
Internet service		
Cable TV		
Gas		
Total =		

Date	Bill	Amount	Jan	Feb	Mar	Apr	May	Jun	Jul	Aug	Sep	Oct	Nov	Dec

Monthly Income: Extra Income: Total Income: Total Paid Out: Cash Available:

Food	Gadgets	Other Expenses

Insurance	Payment	Date Paid

Utilities	Payment	Date Paid
Electricity		
Water		
Sanitation		
Phone service		
Internet service		
Cable TV		
Gas		
Total =		

Date	Bill	Amount	Jan	Feb	Mar	Apr	May	Jun	Jul	Aug	Sep	Oct	Nov	Dec

Monthly Income: Extra Income: Total Income: Total Paid Out: Cash Available:

Food	Gadgets	Other Expenses

Insurance	Payment	Date Paid

Utilities	Payment	Date Paid
Electricity		
Water		
Sanitation		
Phone service		
Internet service		
Cable TV		
Gas		
Total =		

Date	Bill	Amount	Jan	Feb	Mar	Apr	May	Jun	Jul	Aug	Sep	Oct	Nov	Dec

Monthly Income: Extra Income: Total Income: Total Paid Out: Cash Available:

Food	Gadgets	Other Expenses

Insurance	Payment	Date Paid

Utilities	Payment	Date Paid
Electricity		
Water		
Sanitation		
Phone service		
Internet service		
Cable TV		
Gas		
Total =		

Date	Bill	Amount	Jan	Feb	Mar	Apr	May	Jun	Jul	Aug	Sep	Oct	Nov	Dec

Monthly Income: Extra Income: Total Income: Total Paid Out: Cash Available:

Food	Gadgets	Other Expenses

Insurance	Payment	Date Paid

Utilities	Payment	Date Paid
Electricity		
Water		
Sanitation		
Phone service		
Internet service		
Cable TV		
Gas		
Total =		

Date	Bill	Amount	Jan	Feb	Mar	Apr	May	Jun	Jul	Aug	Sep	Oct	Nov	Dec
			☐	☐	☐	☐	☐	☐	☐	☐	☐	☐	☐	☐
			☐	☐	☐	☐	☐	☐	☐	☐	☐	☐	☐	☐
			☐	☐	☐	☐	☐	☐	☐	☐	☐	☐	☐	☐
			☐	☐	☐	☐	☐	☐	☐	☐	☐	☐	☐	☐
			☐	☐	☐	☐	☐	☐	☐	☐	☐	☐	☐	☐
			☐	☐	☐	☐	☐	☐	☐	☐	☐	☐	☐	☐
			☐	☐	☐	☐	☐	☐	☐	☐	☐	☐	☐	☐
			☐	☐	☐	☐	☐	☐	☐	☐	☐	☐	☐	☐
			☐	☐	☐	☐	☐	☐	☐	☐	☐	☐	☐	☐
			☐	☐	☐	☐	☐	☐	☐	☐	☐	☐	☐	☐
			☐	☐	☐	☐	☐	☐	☐	☐	☐	☐	☐	☐
			☐	☐	☐	☐	☐	☐	☐	☐	☐	☐	☐	☐
			☐	☐	☐	☐	☐	☐	☐	☐	☐	☐	☐	☐
			☐	☐	☐	☐	☐	☐	☐	☐	☐	☐	☐	☐

Monthly Income: Extra Income: Total Income: Total Paid Out: Cash Available:

Food	Gadgets	Other Expenses

Insurance	Payment	Date Paid

Utilities	Payment	Date Paid
Electricity		
Water		
Sanitation		
Phone service		
Internet service		
Cable TV		
Gas		
Total =		

Date	Bill	Amount	Jan	Feb	Mar	Apr	May	Jun	Jul	Aug	Sep	Oct	Nov	Dec

Monthly Income: Extra Income: Total Income: Total Paid Out: Cash Available:

Food	Gadgets	Other Expenses

Insurance	Payment	Date Paid

Utilities	Payment	Date Paid
Electricity		
Water		
Sanitation		
Phone service		
Internet service		
Cable TV		
Gas		
Total =		

Date	Bill	Amount	Jan	Feb	Mar	Apr	May	Jun	Jul	Aug	Sep	Oct	Nov	Dec
			☐	☐	☐	☐	☐	☐	☐	☐	☐	☐	☐	☐
			☐	☐	☐	☐	☐	☐	☐	☐	☐	☐	☐	☐
			☐	☐	☐	☐	☐	☐	☐	☐	☐	☐	☐	☐
			☐	☐	☐	☐	☐	☐	☐	☐	☐	☐	☐	☐
			☐	☐	☐	☐	☐	☐	☐	☐	☐	☐	☐	☐
			☐	☐	☐	☐	☐	☐	☐	☐	☐	☐	☐	☐
			☐	☐	☐	☐	☐	☐	☐	☐	☐	☐	☐	☐
			☐	☐	☐	☐	☐	☐	☐	☐	☐	☐	☐	☐
			☐	☐	☐	☐	☐	☐	☐	☐	☐	☐	☐	☐
			☐	☐	☐	☐	☐	☐	☐	☐	☐	☐	☐	☐
			☐	☐	☐	☐	☐	☐	☐	☐	☐	☐	☐	☐
			☐	☐	☐	☐	☐	☐	☐	☐	☐	☐	☐	☐
			☐	☐	☐	☐	☐	☐	☐	☐	☐	☐	☐	☐
			☐	☐	☐	☐	☐	☐	☐	☐	☐	☐	☐	☐

Monthly Income: Extra Income: Total Income: Total Paid Out: Cash Available:

Food	Gadgets	Other Expenses

Insurance	Payment	Date Paid

Utilities	Payment	Date Paid
Electricity		
Water		
Sanitation		
Phone service		
Internet service		
Cable TV		
Gas		
Total =		

Date	Bill	Amount	Jan	Feb	Mar	Apr	May	Jun	Jul	Aug	Sep	Oct	Nov	Dec

Monthly Income: Extra Income: Total Income: Total Paid Out: Cash Available:

Food	Gadgets	Other Expenses

Insurance	Payment	Date Paid

Utilities	Payment	Date Paid
Electricity		
Water		
Sanitation		
Phone service		
Internet service		
Cable TV		
Gas		
Total =		

Date	Bill	Amount	Jan	Feb	Mar	Apr	May	Jun	Jul	Aug	Sep	Oct	Nov	Dec

Monthly Income: Extra Income: Total Income: Total Paid Out: Cash Available:

Food	Gadgets	Other Expenses

Insurance	Payment	Date Paid

Utilities	Payment	Date Paid
Electricity		
Water		
Sanitation		
Phone service		
Internet service		
Cable TV		
Gas		
Total =		

Date	Bill	Amount	Jan	Feb	Mar	Apr	May	Jun	Jul	Aug	Sep	Oct	Nov	Dec

Monthly Income: Extra Income: Total Income: Total Paid Out: Cash Available:

Food	Gadgets	Other Expenses

Insurance	Payment	Date Paid

Utilities	Payment	Date Paid
Electricity		
Water		
Sanitation		
Phone service		
Internet service		
Cable TV		
Gas		
Total =		

Date	Bill	Amount	Jan	Feb	Mar	Apr	May	Jun	Jul	Aug	Sep	Oct	Nov	Dec
			☐	☐	☐	☐	☐	☐	☐	☐	☐	☐	☐	☐
			☐	☐	☐	☐	☐	☐	☐	☐	☐	☐	☐	☐
			☐	☐	☐	☐	☐	☐	☐	☐	☐	☐	☐	☐
			☐	☐	☐	☐	☐	☐	☐	☐	☐	☐	☐	☐
			☐	☐	☐	☐	☐	☐	☐	☐	☐	☐	☐	☐
			☐	☐	☐	☐	☐	☐	☐	☐	☐	☐	☐	☐
			☐	☐	☐	☐	☐	☐	☐	☐	☐	☐	☐	☐
			☐	☐	☐	☐	☐	☐	☐	☐	☐	☐	☐	☐
			☐	☐	☐	☐	☐	☐	☐	☐	☐	☐	☐	☐
			☐	☐	☐	☐	☐	☐	☐	☐	☐	☐	☐	☐
			☐	☐	☐	☐	☐	☐	☐	☐	☐	☐	☐	☐
			☐	☐	☐	☐	☐	☐	☐	☐	☐	☐	☐	☐
			☐	☐	☐	☐	☐	☐	☐	☐	☐	☐	☐	☐
			☐	☐	☐	☐	☐	☐	☐	☐	☐	☐	☐	☐

Monthly Income: Extra Income: Total Income: Total Paid Out: Cash Available:

Food	Gadgets	Other Expenses

Insurance	Payment	Date Paid

Utilities	Payment	Date Paid
Electricity		
Water		
Sanitation		
Phone service		
Internet service		
Cable TV		
Gas		
Total =		

Date	Bill	Amount	Jan	Feb	Mar	Apr	May	Jun	Jul	Aug	Sep	Oct	Nov	Dec

Monthly Income: Extra Income: Total Income: Total Paid Out: Cash Available:

Food	Gadgets	Other Expenses

Insurance	Payment	Date Paid

Utilities	Payment	Date Paid
Electricity		
Water		
Sanitation		
Phone service		
Internet service		
Cable TV		
Gas		
Total =		

Date	Bill	Amount	Jan	Feb	Mar	Apr	May	Jun	Jul	Aug	Sep	Oct	Nov	Dec

Monthly Income: Extra Income: Total Income: Total Paid Out: Cash Available:

Food	Gadgets	Other Expenses

Insurance	Payment	Date Paid

Utilities	Payment	Date Paid
Electricity		
Water		
Sanitation		
Phone service		
Internet service		
Cable TV		
Gas		
Total =		

Date	Bill	Amount	Jan	Feb	Mar	Apr	May	Jun	Jul	Aug	Sep	Oct	Nov	Dec

Monthly Income: Extra Income: Total Income: Total Paid Out: Cash Available:

Food	Gadgets	Other Expenses

Insurance	Payment	Date Paid

Utilities	Payment	Date Paid
Electricity		
Water		
Sanitation		
Phone service		
Internet service		
Cable TV		
Gas		
Total =		

Date	Bill	Amount	Jan	Feb	Mar	Apr	May	Jun	Jul	Aug	Sep	Oct	Nov	Dec

Monthly Income: Extra Income: Total Income: Total Paid Out: Cash Available:

Food	Gadgets	Other Expenses

Insurance	Payment	Date Paid

Utilities	Payment	Date Paid
Electricity		
Water		
Sanitation		
Phone service		
Internet service		
Cable TV		
Gas		
Total =		

Date	Bill	Amount	Jan	Feb	Mar	Apr	May	Jun	Jul	Aug	Sep	Oct	Nov	Dec

Monthly Income: Extra Income: Total Income: Total Paid Out: Cash Available:

Food	Gadgets	Other Expenses

Insurance	Payment	Date Paid

Utilities	Payment	Date Paid
Electricity		
Water		
Sanitation		
Phone service		
Internet service		
Cable TV		
Gas		
Total =		

Date	Bill	Amount	Jan	Feb	Mar	Apr	May	Jun	Jul	Aug	Sep	Oct	Nov	Dec

Monthly Income: Extra Income: Total Income: Total Paid Out: Cash Available:

Food	Gadgets	Other Expenses

Insurance	Payment	Date Paid

Utilities	Payment	Date Paid
Electricity		
Water		
Sanitation		
Phone service		
Internet service		
Cable TV		
Gas		
Total =		

Date	Bill	Amount	Jan	Feb	Mar	Apr	May	Jun	Jul	Aug	Sep	Oct	Nov	Dec

Monthly Income: Extra Income: Total Income: Total Paid Out: Cash Available:

Food	Gadgets	Other Expenses

Insurance	Payment	Date Paid

Utilities	Payment	Date Paid
Electricity		
Water		
Sanitation		
Phone service		
Internet service		
Cable TV		
Gas		
Total =		

Date	Bill	Amount	Jan	Feb	Mar	Apr	May	Jun	Jul	Aug	Sep	Oct	Nov	Dec
			☐	☐	☐	☐	☐	☐	☐	☐	☐	☐	☐	☐
			☐	☐	☐	☐	☐	☐	☐	☐	☐	☐	☐	☐
			☐	☐	☐	☐	☐	☐	☐	☐	☐	☐	☐	☐
			☐	☐	☐	☐	☐	☐	☐	☐	☐	☐	☐	☐
			☐	☐	☐	☐	☐	☐	☐	☐	☐	☐	☐	☐
			☐	☐	☐	☐	☐	☐	☐	☐	☐	☐	☐	☐
			☐	☐	☐	☐	☐	☐	☐	☐	☐	☐	☐	☐
			☐	☐	☐	☐	☐	☐	☐	☐	☐	☐	☐	☐
			☐	☐	☐	☐	☐	☐	☐	☐	☐	☐	☐	☐
			☐	☐	☐	☐	☐	☐	☐	☐	☐	☐	☐	☐
			☐	☐	☐	☐	☐	☐	☐	☐	☐	☐	☐	☐
			☐	☐	☐	☐	☐	☐	☐	☐	☐	☐	☐	☐
			☐	☐	☐	☐	☐	☐	☐	☐	☐	☐	☐	☐
			☐	☐	☐	☐	☐	☐	☐	☐	☐	☐	☐	☐

Monthly Income: Extra Income: Total Income: Total Paid Out: Cash Available:

Food	Gadgets	Other Expenses

Insurance	Payment	Date Paid

Utilities	Payment	Date Paid
Electricity		
Water		
Sanitation		
Phone service		
Internet service		
Cable TV		
Gas		
Total =		

Date	Bill	Amount	Jan	Feb	Mar	Apr	May	Jun	Jul	Aug	Sep	Oct	Nov	Dec
			☐	☐	☐	☐	☐	☐	☐	☐	☐	☐	☐	☐
			☐	☐	☐	☐	☐	☐	☐	☐	☐	☐	☐	☐
			☐	☐	☐	☐	☐	☐	☐	☐	☐	☐	☐	☐
			☐	☐	☐	☐	☐	☐	☐	☐	☐	☐	☐	☐
			☐	☐	☐	☐	☐	☐	☐	☐	☐	☐	☐	☐
			☐	☐	☐	☐	☐	☐	☐	☐	☐	☐	☐	☐
			☐	☐	☐	☐	☐	☐	☐	☐	☐	☐	☐	☐
			☐	☐	☐	☐	☐	☐	☐	☐	☐	☐	☐	☐
			☐	☐	☐	☐	☐	☐	☐	☐	☐	☐	☐	☐
			☐	☐	☐	☐	☐	☐	☐	☐	☐	☐	☐	☐
			☐	☐	☐	☐	☐	☐	☐	☐	☐	☐	☐	☐
			☐	☐	☐	☐	☐	☐	☐	☐	☐	☐	☐	☐
			☐	☐	☐	☐	☐	☐	☐	☐	☐	☐	☐	☐
			☐	☐	☐	☐	☐	☐	☐	☐	☐	☐	☐	☐

Monthly Income: Extra Income: Total Income: Total Paid Out: Cash Available:

Food	Gadgets	Other Expenses

Insurance	Payment	Date Paid

Utilities	Payment	Date Paid
Electricity		
Water		
Sanitation		
Phone service		
Internet service		
Cable TV		
Gas		
Total =		

Date	Bill	Amount	Jan	Feb	Mar	Apr	May	Jun	Jul	Aug	Sep	Oct	Nov	Dec

Monthly Income: Extra Income: Total Income: Total Paid Out: Cash Available:

Food	Gadgets	Other Expenses

Insurance	Payment	Date Paid

Utilities	Payment	Date Paid
Electricity		
Water		
Sanitation		
Phone service		
Internet service		
Cable TV		
Gas		
Total =		

Date	Bill	Amount	Jan	Feb	Mar	Apr	May	Jun	Jul	Aug	Sep	Oct	Nov	Dec

Monthly Income: Extra Income: Total Income: Total Paid Out: Cash Available:

Food	Gadgets	Other Expenses

Insurance	Payment	Date Paid

Utilities	Payment	Date Paid
Electricity		
Water		
Sanitation		
Phone service		
Internet service		
Cable TV		
Gas		
Total =		

Date	Bill	Amount	Jan	Feb	Mar	Apr	May	Jun	Jul	Aug	Sep	Oct	Nov	Dec

Monthly Income: Extra Income: Total Income: Total Paid Out: Cash Available:

Food	Gadgets	Other Expenses

Insurance	Payment	Date Paid

Utilities	Payment	Date Paid
Electricity		
Water		
Sanitation		
Phone service		
Internet service		
Cable TV		
Gas		
Total =		

Date	Bill	Amount	Jan	Feb	Mar	Apr	May	Jun	Jul	Aug	Sep	Oct	Nov	Dec

Monthly Income: Extra Income: Total Income: Total Paid Out: Cash Available:

Food	Gadgets	Other Expenses

Insurance	Payment	Date Paid

Utilities	Payment	Date Paid
Electricity		
Water		
Sanitation		
Phone service		
Internet service		
Cable TV		
Gas		
Total =		

Date	Bill	Amount	Jan	Feb	Mar	Apr	May	Jun	Jul	Aug	Sep	Oct	Nov	Dec
____	____	____	☐	☐	☐	☐	☐	☐	☐	☐	☐	☐	☐	☐
____	____	____	☐	☐	☐	☐	☐	☐	☐	☐	☐	☐	☐	☐
____	____	____	☐	☐	☐	☐	☐	☐	☐	☐	☐	☐	☐	☐
____	____	____	☐	☐	☐	☐	☐	☐	☐	☐	☐	☐	☐	☐
____	____	____	☐	☐	☐	☐	☐	☐	☐	☐	☐	☐	☐	☐
____	____	____	☐	☐	☐	☐	☐	☐	☐	☐	☐	☐	☐	☐
____	____	____	☐	☐	☐	☐	☐	☐	☐	☐	☐	☐	☐	☐
____	____	____	☐	☐	☐	☐	☐	☐	☐	☐	☐	☐	☐	☐
____	____	____	☐	☐	☐	☐	☐	☐	☐	☐	☐	☐	☐	☐
____	____	____	☐	☐	☐	☐	☐	☐	☐	☐	☐	☐	☐	☐
____	____	____	☐	☐	☐	☐	☐	☐	☐	☐	☐	☐	☐	☐
____	____	____	☐	☐	☐	☐	☐	☐	☐	☐	☐	☐	☐	☐
____	____	____	☐	☐	☐	☐	☐	☐	☐	☐	☐	☐	☐	☐
____	____	____	☐	☐	☐	☐	☐	☐	☐	☐	☐	☐	☐	☐
____	____	____	☐	☐	☐	☐	☐	☐	☐	☐	☐	☐	☐	☐

Monthly Income: Extra Income: Total Income: Total Paid Out: Cash Available:

Food	Gadgets	Other Expenses

Insurance	Payment	Date Paid

Utilities	Payment	Date Paid
Electricity		
Water		
Sanitation		
Phone service		
Internet service		
Cable TV		
Gas		
Total =		

Date	Bill	Amount	Jan	Feb	Mar	Apr	May	Jun	Jul	Aug	Sep	Oct	Nov	Dec

Monthly Income: Extra Income: Total Income: Total Paid Out: Cash Available:

Food	Gadgets	Other Expenses

Insurance	Payment	Date Paid

Utilities	Payment	Date Paid
Electricity		
Water		
Sanitation		
Phone service		
Internet service		
Cable TV		
Gas		
Total =		

Date	Bill	Amount	Jan	Feb	Mar	Apr	May	Jun	Jul	Aug	Sep	Oct	Nov	Dec

Monthly Income: Extra Income: Total Income: Total Paid Out: Cash Available:

Food	Gadgets	Other Expenses

Insurance	Payment	Date Paid

Utilities	Payment	Date Paid
Electricity		
Water		
Sanitation		
Phone service		
Internet service		
Cable TV		
Gas		
Total =		

Date	Bill	Amount	Jan	Feb	Mar	Apr	May	Jun	Jul	Aug	Sep	Oct	Nov	Dec

Monthly Income: Extra Income: Total Income: Total Paid Out: Cash Available:

Food	Gadgets	Other Expenses

Insurance	Payment	Date Paid

Utilities	Payment	Date Paid
Electricity		
Water		
Sanitation		
Phone service		
Internet service		
Cable TV		
Gas		
Total =		

Date	Bill	Amount	Jan	Feb	Mar	Apr	May	Jun	Jul	Aug	Sep	Oct	Nov	Dec
			☐	☐	☐	☐	☐	☐	☐	☐	☐	☐	☐	☐
			☐	☐	☐	☐	☐	☐	☐	☐	☐	☐	☐	☐
			☐	☐	☐	☐	☐	☐	☐	☐	☐	☐	☐	☐
			☐	☐	☐	☐	☐	☐	☐	☐	☐	☐	☐	☐
			☐	☐	☐	☐	☐	☐	☐	☐	☐	☐	☐	☐
			☐	☐	☐	☐	☐	☐	☐	☐	☐	☐	☐	☐
			☐	☐	☐	☐	☐	☐	☐	☐	☐	☐	☐	☐
			☐	☐	☐	☐	☐	☐	☐	☐	☐	☐	☐	☐
			☐	☐	☐	☐	☐	☐	☐	☐	☐	☐	☐	☐
			☐	☐	☐	☐	☐	☐	☐	☐	☐	☐	☐	☐
			☐	☐	☐	☐	☐	☐	☐	☐	☐	☐	☐	☐
			☐	☐	☐	☐	☐	☐	☐	☐	☐	☐	☐	☐
			☐	☐	☐	☐	☐	☐	☐	☐	☐	☐	☐	☐
			☐	☐	☐	☐	☐	☐	☐	☐	☐	☐	☐	☐

Monthly Income: Extra Income: Total Income: Total Paid Out: Cash Available:

Food	Gadgets	Other Expenses

Insurance	Payment	Date Paid

Utilities	Payment	Date Paid
Electricity		
Water		
Sanitation		
Phone service		
Internet service		
Cable TV		
Gas		
Total =		

Date	Bill	Amount	Jan	Feb	Mar	Apr	May	Jun	Jul	Aug	Sep	Oct	Nov	Dec

Monthly Income: Extra Income: Total Income: Total Paid Out: Cash Available:

Food	Gadgets	Other Expenses

Insurance	Payment	Date Paid

Utilities	Payment	Date Paid
Electricity		
Water		
Sanitation		
Phone service		
Internet service		
Cable TV		
Gas		
Total =		

Date	Bill	Amount	Jan	Feb	Mar	Apr	May	Jun	Jul	Aug	Sep	Oct	Nov	Dec

Monthly Income: Extra Income: Total Income: Total Paid Out: Cash Available:

Food	Gadgets	Other Expenses

Insurance	Payment	Date Paid

Utilities	Payment	Date Paid
Electricity		
Water		
Sanitation		
Phone service		
Internet service		
Cable TV		
Gas		
Total =		

Date	Bill	Amount	Jan	Feb	Mar	Apr	May	Jun	Jul	Aug	Sep	Oct	Nov	Dec
			☐	☐	☐	☐	☐	☐	☐	☐	☐	☐	☐	☐
			☐	☐	☐	☐	☐	☐	☐	☐	☐	☐	☐	☐
			☐	☐	☐	☐	☐	☐	☐	☐	☐	☐	☐	☐
			☐	☐	☐	☐	☐	☐	☐	☐	☐	☐	☐	☐
			☐	☐	☐	☐	☐	☐	☐	☐	☐	☐	☐	☐
			☐	☐	☐	☐	☐	☐	☐	☐	☐	☐	☐	☐
			☐	☐	☐	☐	☐	☐	☐	☐	☐	☐	☐	☐
			☐	☐	☐	☐	☐	☐	☐	☐	☐	☐	☐	☐
			☐	☐	☐	☐	☐	☐	☐	☐	☐	☐	☐	☐
			☐	☐	☐	☐	☐	☐	☐	☐	☐	☐	☐	☐
			☐	☐	☐	☐	☐	☐	☐	☐	☐	☐	☐	☐
			☐	☐	☐	☐	☐	☐	☐	☐	☐	☐	☐	☐
			☐	☐	☐	☐	☐	☐	☐	☐	☐	☐	☐	☐

Monthly Income: Extra Income: Total Income: Total Paid Out: Cash Available:

Food	Gadgets	Other Expenses

Insurance	Payment	Date Paid

Utilities	Payment	Date Paid
Electricity		
Water		
Sanitation		
Phone service		
Internet service		
Cable TV		
Gas		
Total =		

Date	Bill	Amount	Jan	Feb	Mar	Apr	May	Jun	Jul	Aug	Sep	Oct	Nov	Dec

Monthly Income: Extra Income: Total Income: Total Paid Out: Cash Available:

Food	Gadgets	Other Expenses

Insurance	Payment	Date Paid

Utilities	Payment	Date Paid
Electricity		
Water		
Sanitation		
Phone service		
Internet service		
Cable TV		
Gas		
Total =		

Date	Bill	Amount	Jan	Feb	Mar	Apr	May	Jun	Jul	Aug	Sep	Oct	Nov	Dec

Monthly Income: Extra Income: Total Income: Total Paid Out: Cash Available:

Food	Gadgets	Other Expenses

Insurance	Payment	Date Paid

Utilities	Payment	Date Paid
Electricity		
Water		
Sanitation		
Phone service		
Internet service		
Cable TV		
Gas		
Total =		

Date	Bill	Amount	Jan	Feb	Mar	Apr	May	Jun	Jul	Aug	Sep	Oct	Nov	Dec

Monthly Income: Extra Income: Total Income: Total Paid Out: Cash Available:

Food	Gadgets	Other Expenses

Insurance	Payment	Date Paid

Utilities	Payment	Date Paid
Electricity		
Water		
Sanitation		
Phone service		
Internet service		
Cable TV		
Gas		
Total =		

Date	Bill	Amount	Jan	Feb	Mar	Apr	May	Jun	Jul	Aug	Sep	Oct	Nov	Dec

Monthly Income: Extra Income: Total Income: Total Paid Out: Cash Available:

Food	Gadgets	Other Expenses

Insurance	Payment	Date Paid

Utilities	Payment	Date Paid
Electricity		
Water		
Sanitation		
Phone service		
Internet service		
Cable TV		
Gas		
Total =		

Date	Bill	Amount	Jan	Feb	Mar	Apr	May	Jun	Jul	Aug	Sep	Oct	Nov	Dec

Monthly Income: Extra Income: Total Income: Total Paid Out: Cash Available:

Food	Gadgets	Other Expenses

Insurance	Payment	Date Paid

Utilities	Payment	Date Paid
Electricity		
Water		
Sanitation		
Phone service		
Internet service		
Cable TV		
Gas		
Total =		

Date	Bill	Amount	Jan	Feb	Mar	Apr	May	Jun	Jul	Aug	Sep	Oct	Nov	Dec

Monthly Income: Extra Income: Total Income: Total Paid Out: Cash Available:

Food	Gadgets	Other Expenses

Insurance	Payment	Date Paid

Utilities	Payment	Date Paid
Electricity		
Water		
Sanitation		
Phone service		
Internet service		
Cable TV		
Gas		
Total =		

Date	Bill	Amount	Jan	Feb	Mar	Apr	May	Jun	Jul	Aug	Sep	Oct	Nov	Dec

Monthly Income: Extra Income: Total Income: Total Paid Out: Cash Available:

Food	Gadgets	Other Expenses

Insurance	Payment	Date Paid

Utilities	Payment	Date Paid
Electricity		
Water		
Sanitation		
Phone service		
Internet service		
Cable TV		
Gas		
Total =		

Date	Bill	Amount	Jan	Feb	Mar	Apr	May	Jun	Jul	Aug	Sep	Oct	Nov	Dec

Monthly Income: Extra Income: Total Income: Total Paid Out: Cash Available:

Food	Gadgets	Other Expenses

Insurance	Payment	Date Paid

Utilities	Payment	Date Paid
Electricity		
Water		
Sanitation		
Phone service		
Internet service		
Cable TV		
Gas		
Total =		

Date	Bill	Amount	Jan	Feb	Mar	Apr	May	Jun	Jul	Aug	Sep	Oct	Nov	Dec

Monthly Income: Extra Income: Total Income: Total Paid Out: Cash Available:

Food	Gadgets	Other Expenses

Insurance	Payment	Date Paid

Utilities	Payment	Date Paid
Electricity		
Water		
Sanitation		
Phone service		
Internet service		
Cable TV		
Gas		
Total =		

Date	Bill	Amount	Jan	Feb	Mar	Apr	May	Jun	Jul	Aug	Sep	Oct	Nov	Dec

Monthly Income: Extra Income: Total Income: Total Paid Out: Cash Available:

Food	Gadgets	Other Expenses

Insurance	Payment	Date Paid

Utilities	Payment	Date Paid
Electricity		
Water		
Sanitation		
Phone service		
Internet service		
Cable TV		
Gas		
Total =		

Date	Bill	Amount	Jan	Feb	Mar	Apr	May	Jun	Jul	Aug	Sep	Oct	Nov	Dec

Monthly Income: Extra Income: Total Income: Total Paid Out: Cash Available:

Food	Gadgets	Other Expenses

Insurance	Payment	Date Paid

Utilities	Payment	Date Paid
Electricity		
Water		
Sanitation		
Phone service		
Internet service		
Cable TV		
Gas		
Total =		

Date	Bill	Amount	Jan	Feb	Mar	Apr	May	Jun	Jul	Aug	Sep	Oct	Nov	Dec

Monthly Income: Extra Income: Total Income: Total Paid Out: Cash Available:

Food	Gadgets	Other Expenses

Insurance	Payment	Date Paid

Utilities	Payment	Date Paid
Electricity		
Water		
Sanitation		
Phone service		
Internet service		
Cable TV		
Gas		
Total =		

Date	Bill	Amount	Jan	Feb	Mar	Apr	May	Jun	Jul	Aug	Sep	Oct	Nov	Dec
			☐	☐	☐	☐	☐	☐	☐	☐	☐	☐	☐	☐
			☐	☐	☐	☐	☐	☐	☐	☐	☐	☐	☐	☐
			☐	☐	☐	☐	☐	☐	☐	☐	☐	☐	☐	☐
			☐	☐	☐	☐	☐	☐	☐	☐	☐	☐	☐	☐
			☐	☐	☐	☐	☐	☐	☐	☐	☐	☐	☐	☐
			☐	☐	☐	☐	☐	☐	☐	☐	☐	☐	☐	☐
			☐	☐	☐	☐	☐	☐	☐	☐	☐	☐	☐	☐
			☐	☐	☐	☐	☐	☐	☐	☐	☐	☐	☐	☐
			☐	☐	☐	☐	☐	☐	☐	☐	☐	☐	☐	☐
			☐	☐	☐	☐	☐	☐	☐	☐	☐	☐	☐	☐
			☐	☐	☐	☐	☐	☐	☐	☐	☐	☐	☐	☐
			☐	☐	☐	☐	☐	☐	☐	☐	☐	☐	☐	☐
			☐	☐	☐	☐	☐	☐	☐	☐	☐	☐	☐	☐
			☐	☐	☐	☐	☐	☐	☐	☐	☐	☐	☐	☐

Monthly Income: Extra Income: Total Income: Total Paid Out: Cash Available:

Food	Gadgets	Other Expenses

Insurance	Payment	Date Paid

Utilities	Payment	Date Paid
Electricity		
Water		
Sanitation		
Phone service		
Internet service		
Cable TV		
Gas		
Total =		

Date	Bill	Amount	Jan	Feb	Mar	Apr	May	Jun	Jul	Aug	Sep	Oct	Nov	Dec
			☐	☐	☐	☐	☐	☐	☐	☐	☐	☐	☐	☐
			☐	☐	☐	☐	☐	☐	☐	☐	☐	☐	☐	☐
			☐	☐	☐	☐	☐	☐	☐	☐	☐	☐	☐	☐
			☐	☐	☐	☐	☐	☐	☐	☐	☐	☐	☐	☐
			☐	☐	☐	☐	☐	☐	☐	☐	☐	☐	☐	☐
			☐	☐	☐	☐	☐	☐	☐	☐	☐	☐	☐	☐
			☐	☐	☐	☐	☐	☐	☐	☐	☐	☐	☐	☐
			☐	☐	☐	☐	☐	☐	☐	☐	☐	☐	☐	☐
			☐	☐	☐	☐	☐	☐	☐	☐	☐	☐	☐	☐
			☐	☐	☐	☐	☐	☐	☐	☐	☐	☐	☐	☐
			☐	☐	☐	☐	☐	☐	☐	☐	☐	☐	☐	☐
			☐	☐	☐	☐	☐	☐	☐	☐	☐	☐	☐	☐
			☐	☐	☐	☐	☐	☐	☐	☐	☐	☐	☐	☐
			☐	☐	☐	☐	☐	☐	☐	☐	☐	☐	☐	☐

Monthly Income: Extra Income: Total Income: Total Paid Out: Cash Available:

Food	Gadgets	Other Expenses

Insurance	Payment	Date Paid

Utilities	Payment	Date Paid
Electricity		
Water		
Sanitation		
Phone service		
Internet service		
Cable TV		
Gas		
Total =		

Date	Bill	Amount	Jan	Feb	Mar	Apr	May	Jun	Jul	Aug	Sep	Oct	Nov	Dec
______	______	______	☐	☐	☐	☐	☐	☐	☐	☐	☐	☐	☐	☐
______	______	______	☐	☐	☐	☐	☐	☐	☐	☐	☐	☐	☐	☐
______	______	______	☐	☐	☐	☐	☐	☐	☐	☐	☐	☐	☐	☐
______	______	______	☐	☐	☐	☐	☐	☐	☐	☐	☐	☐	☐	☐
______	______	______	☐	☐	☐	☐	☐	☐	☐	☐	☐	☐	☐	☐
______	______	______	☐	☐	☐	☐	☐	☐	☐	☐	☐	☐	☐	☐
______	______	______	☐	☐	☐	☐	☐	☐	☐	☐	☐	☐	☐	☐
______	______	______	☐	☐	☐	☐	☐	☐	☐	☐	☐	☐	☐	☐
______	______	______	☐	☐	☐	☐	☐	☐	☐	☐	☐	☐	☐	☐
______	______	______	☐	☐	☐	☐	☐	☐	☐	☐	☐	☐	☐	☐
______	______	______	☐	☐	☐	☐	☐	☐	☐	☐	☐	☐	☐	☐
______	______	______	☐	☐	☐	☐	☐	☐	☐	☐	☐	☐	☐	☐
______	______	______	☐	☐	☐	☐	☐	☐	☐	☐	☐	☐	☐	☐
______	______	______	☐	☐	☐	☐	☐	☐	☐	☐	☐	☐	☐	☐

Monthly Income: Extra Income: Total Income: Total Paid Out: Cash Available:

Food	Gadgets	Other Expenses

Insurance	Payment	Date Paid

Utilities	Payment	Date Paid
Electricity		
Water		
Sanitation		
Phone service		
Internet service		
Cable TV		
Gas		
Total =		

Date	Bill	Amount	Jan	Feb	Mar	Apr	May	Jun	Jul	Aug	Sep	Oct	Nov	Dec

Monthly Income: Extra Income: Total Income: Total Paid Out: Cash Available:

Food	Gadgets	Other Expenses

Insurance	Payment	Date Paid

Utilities	Payment	Date Paid
Electricity		
Water		
Sanitation		
Phone service		
Internet service		
Cable TV		
Gas		
Total =		

Date	Bill	Amount	Jan	Feb	Mar	Apr	May	Jun	Jul	Aug	Sep	Oct	Nov	Dec
___	___	___												
___	___	___												
___	___	___												
___	___	___												
___	___	___												
___	___	___												
___	___	___												
___	___	___												
___	___	___												
___	___	___												
___	___	___												
___	___	___												
___	___	___												
___	___	___												

Monthly Income: Extra Income: Total Income: Total Paid Out: Cash Available:

Food	Gadgets	Other Expenses

Insurance	Payment	Date Paid

Utilities	Payment	Date Paid
Electricity		
Water		
Sanitation		
Phone service		
Internet service		
Cable TV		
Gas		
Total =		

Date	Bill	Amount	Jan	Feb	Mar	Apr	May	Jun	Jul	Aug	Sep	Oct	Nov	Dec

Monthly Income: Extra Income: Total Income: Total Paid Out: Cash Available:

Food	Gadgets	Other Expenses

Insurance	Payment	Date Paid

Utilities	Payment	Date Paid
Electricity		
Water		
Sanitation		
Phone service		
Internet service		
Cable TV		
Gas		
Total =		

Date	Bill	Amount	Jan	Feb	Mar	Apr	May	Jun	Jul	Aug	Sep	Oct	Nov	Dec

Monthly Income: Extra Income: Total Income: Total Paid Out: Cash Available:

Food	Gadgets	Other Expenses

Insurance	Payment	Date Paid

Utilities	Payment	Date Paid
Electricity		
Water		
Sanitation		
Phone service		
Internet service		
Cable TV		
Gas		
Total =		

Date	Bill	Amount	Jan	Feb	Mar	Apr	May	Jun	Jul	Aug	Sep	Oct	Nov	Dec
			☐	☐	☐	☐	☐	☐	☐	☐	☐	☐	☐	☐
			☐	☐	☐	☐	☐	☐	☐	☐	☐	☐	☐	☐
			☐	☐	☐	☐	☐	☐	☐	☐	☐	☐	☐	☐
			☐	☐	☐	☐	☐	☐	☐	☐	☐	☐	☐	☐
			☐	☐	☐	☐	☐	☐	☐	☐	☐	☐	☐	☐
			☐	☐	☐	☐	☐	☐	☐	☐	☐	☐	☐	☐
			☐	☐	☐	☐	☐	☐	☐	☐	☐	☐	☐	☐
			☐	☐	☐	☐	☐	☐	☐	☐	☐	☐	☐	☐
			☐	☐	☐	☐	☐	☐	☐	☐	☐	☐	☐	☐
			☐	☐	☐	☐	☐	☐	☐	☐	☐	☐	☐	☐
			☐	☐	☐	☐	☐	☐	☐	☐	☐	☐	☐	☐
			☐	☐	☐	☐	☐	☐	☐	☐	☐	☐	☐	☐
			☐	☐	☐	☐	☐	☐	☐	☐	☐	☐	☐	☐
			☐	☐	☐	☐	☐	☐	☐	☐	☐	☐	☐	☐

Monthly Income: Extra Income: Total Income: Total Paid Out: Cash Available:

Food	Gadgets	Other Expenses

Insurance	Payment	Date Paid

Utilities	Payment	Date Paid
Electricity		
Water		
Sanitation		
Phone service		
Internet service		
Cable TV		
Gas		
Total =		

Date	Bill	Amount	Jan	Feb	Mar	Apr	May	Jun	Jul	Aug	Sep	Oct	Nov	Dec

Monthly Income: Extra Income: Total Income: Total Paid Out: Cash Available:

Food	Gadgets	Other Expenses

Insurance	Payment	Date Paid

Utilities	Payment	Date Paid
Electricity		
Water		
Sanitation		
Phone service		
Internet service		
Cable TV		
Gas		
Total =		

Date	Bill	Amount	Jan	Feb	Mar	Apr	May	Jun	Jul	Aug	Sep	Oct	Nov	Dec

Monthly Income: Extra Income: Total Income: Total Paid Out: Cash Available:

Food	Gadgets	Other Expenses

Insurance	Payment	Date Paid

Utilities	Payment	Date Paid
Electricity		
Water		
Sanitation		
Phone service		
Internet service		
Cable TV		
Gas		
Total =		

Date	Bill	Amount	Jan	Feb	Mar	Apr	May	Jun	Jul	Aug	Sep	Oct	Nov	Dec
			☐	☐	☐	☐	☐	☐	☐	☐	☐	☐	☐	☐
			☐	☐	☐	☐	☐	☐	☐	☐	☐	☐	☐	☐
			☐	☐	☐	☐	☐	☐	☐	☐	☐	☐	☐	☐
			☐	☐	☐	☐	☐	☐	☐	☐	☐	☐	☐	☐
			☐	☐	☐	☐	☐	☐	☐	☐	☐	☐	☐	☐
			☐	☐	☐	☐	☐	☐	☐	☐	☐	☐	☐	☐
			☐	☐	☐	☐	☐	☐	☐	☐	☐	☐	☐	☐
			☐	☐	☐	☐	☐	☐	☐	☐	☐	☐	☐	☐
			☐	☐	☐	☐	☐	☐	☐	☐	☐	☐	☐	☐
			☐	☐	☐	☐	☐	☐	☐	☐	☐	☐	☐	☐
			☐	☐	☐	☐	☐	☐	☐	☐	☐	☐	☐	☐
			☐	☐	☐	☐	☐	☐	☐	☐	☐	☐	☐	☐
			☐	☐	☐	☐	☐	☐	☐	☐	☐	☐	☐	☐
			☐	☐	☐	☐	☐	☐	☐	☐	☐	☐	☐	☐
			☐	☐	☐	☐	☐	☐	☐	☐	☐	☐	☐	☐

Monthly Income: Extra Income: Total Income: Total Paid Out: Cash Available:

Food	Gadgets	Other Expenses

Insurance	Payment	Date Paid

Utilities	Payment	Date Paid
Electricity		
Water		
Sanitation		
Phone service		
Internet service		
Cable TV		
Gas		
Total =		

Date	Bill	Amount	Jan	Feb	Mar	Apr	May	Jun	Jul	Aug	Sep	Oct	Nov	Dec

Monthly Income: Extra Income: Total Income: Total Paid Out: Cash Available:

Food	Gadgets	Other Expenses

Insurance	Payment	Date Paid

Utilities	Payment	Date Paid
Electricity		
Water		
Sanitation		
Phone service		
Internet service		
Cable TV		
Gas		
Total =		

Date	Bill	Amount	Jan	Feb	Mar	Apr	May	Jun	Jul	Aug	Sep	Oct	Nov	Dec
___	___	___	☐	☐	☐	☐	☐	☐	☐	☐	☐	☐	☐	☐
___	___	___	☐	☐	☐	☐	☐	☐	☐	☐	☐	☐	☐	☐
___	___	___	☐	☐	☐	☐	☐	☐	☐	☐	☐	☐	☐	☐
___	___	___	☐	☐	☐	☐	☐	☐	☐	☐	☐	☐	☐	☐
___	___	___	☐	☐	☐	☐	☐	☐	☐	☐	☐	☐	☐	☐
___	___	___	☐	☐	☐	☐	☐	☐	☐	☐	☐	☐	☐	☐
___	___	___	☐	☐	☐	☐	☐	☐	☐	☐	☐	☐	☐	☐
___	___	___	☐	☐	☐	☐	☐	☐	☐	☐	☐	☐	☐	☐
___	___	___	☐	☐	☐	☐	☐	☐	☐	☐	☐	☐	☐	☐
___	___	___	☐	☐	☐	☐	☐	☐	☐	☐	☐	☐	☐	☐
___	___	___	☐	☐	☐	☐	☐	☐	☐	☐	☐	☐	☐	☐
___	___	___	☐	☐	☐	☐	☐	☐	☐	☐	☐	☐	☐	☐
___	___	___	☐	☐	☐	☐	☐	☐	☐	☐	☐	☐	☐	☐

Monthly Income: Extra Income: Total Income: Total Paid Out: Cash Available:

Food	Gadgets	Other Expenses

Insurance	Payment	Date Paid

Utilities	Payment	Date Paid
Electricity		
Water		
Sanitation		
Phone service		
Internet service		
Cable TV		
Gas		
Total =		

Date	Bill	Amount	Jan	Feb	Mar	Apr	May	Jun	Jul	Aug	Sep	Oct	Nov	Dec
			☐	☐	☐	☐	☐	☐	☐	☐	☐	☐	☐	☐
			☐	☐	☐	☐	☐	☐	☐	☐	☐	☐	☐	☐
			☐	☐	☐	☐	☐	☐	☐	☐	☐	☐	☐	☐
			☐	☐	☐	☐	☐	☐	☐	☐	☐	☐	☐	☐
			☐	☐	☐	☐	☐	☐	☐	☐	☐	☐	☐	☐
			☐	☐	☐	☐	☐	☐	☐	☐	☐	☐	☐	☐
			☐	☐	☐	☐	☐	☐	☐	☐	☐	☐	☐	☐
			☐	☐	☐	☐	☐	☐	☐	☐	☐	☐	☐	☐
			☐	☐	☐	☐	☐	☐	☐	☐	☐	☐	☐	☐
			☐	☐	☐	☐	☐	☐	☐	☐	☐	☐	☐	☐
			☐	☐	☐	☐	☐	☐	☐	☐	☐	☐	☐	☐
			☐	☐	☐	☐	☐	☐	☐	☐	☐	☐	☐	☐
			☐	☐	☐	☐	☐	☐	☐	☐	☐	☐	☐	☐
			☐	☐	☐	☐	☐	☐	☐	☐	☐	☐	☐	☐

Monthly Income: Extra Income: Total Income: Total Paid Out: Cash Available:

Food	Gadgets	Other Expenses

Insurance	Payment	Date Paid

Utilities	Payment	Date Paid
Electricity		
Water		
Sanitation		
Phone service		
Internet service		
Cable TV		
Gas		
Total =		

Date	Bill	Amount	Jan	Feb	Mar	Apr	May	Jun	Jul	Aug	Sep	Oct	Nov	Dec
___	___	___	☐	☐	☐	☐	☐	☐	☐	☐	☐	☐	☐	☐
___	___	___	☐	☐	☐	☐	☐	☐	☐	☐	☐	☐	☐	☐
___	___	___	☐	☐	☐	☐	☐	☐	☐	☐	☐	☐	☐	☐
___	___	___	☐	☐	☐	☐	☐	☐	☐	☐	☐	☐	☐	☐
___	___	___	☐	☐	☐	☐	☐	☐	☐	☐	☐	☐	☐	☐
___	___	___	☐	☐	☐	☐	☐	☐	☐	☐	☐	☐	☐	☐
___	___	___	☐	☐	☐	☐	☐	☐	☐	☐	☐	☐	☐	☐
___	___	___	☐	☐	☐	☐	☐	☐	☐	☐	☐	☐	☐	☐
___	___	___	☐	☐	☐	☐	☐	☐	☐	☐	☐	☐	☐	☐
___	___	___	☐	☐	☐	☐	☐	☐	☐	☐	☐	☐	☐	☐
___	___	___	☐	☐	☐	☐	☐	☐	☐	☐	☐	☐	☐	☐
___	___	___	☐	☐	☐	☐	☐	☐	☐	☐	☐	☐	☐	☐
___	___	___	☐	☐	☐	☐	☐	☐	☐	☐	☐	☐	☐	☐
___	___	___	☐	☐	☐	☐	☐	☐	☐	☐	☐	☐	☐	☐
___	___	___	☐	☐	☐	☐	☐	☐	☐	☐	☐	☐	☐	☐

Monthly Income: Extra Income: Total Income: Total Paid Out: Cash Available:

Food	Gadgets	Other Expenses

Insurance	Payment	Date Paid

Utilities	Payment	Date Paid
Electricity		
Water		
Sanitation		
Phone service		
Internet service		
Cable TV		
Gas		
Total =		

Date	Bill	Amount	Jan	Feb	Mar	Apr	May	Jun	Jul	Aug	Sep	Oct	Nov	Dec

Monthly Income: Extra Income: Total Income: Total Paid Out: Cash Available:

Food	Gadgets	Other Expenses

Insurance	Payment	Date Paid

Utilities	Payment	Date Paid
Electricity		
Water		
Sanitation		
Phone service		
Internet service		
Cable TV		
Gas		
Total =		

Date	Bill	Amount	Jan	Feb	Mar	Apr	May	Jun	Jul	Aug	Sep	Oct	Nov	Dec

Monthly Income: Extra Income: Total Income: Total Paid Out: Cash Available:

Food	Gadgets	Other Expenses

Insurance	Payment	Date Paid

Utilities	Payment	Date Paid
Electricity		
Water		
Sanitation		
Phone service		
Internet service		
Cable TV		
Gas		
Total =		

Date	Bill	Amount	Jan	Feb	Mar	Apr	May	Jun	Jul	Aug	Sep	Oct	Nov	Dec

Monthly Income: Extra Income: Total Income: Total Paid Out: Cash Available:

Food	Gadgets	Other Expenses

Insurance	Payment	Date Paid

Utilities	Payment	Date Paid
Electricity		
Water		
Sanitation		
Phone service		
Internet service		
Cable TV		
Gas		
Total =		

Date	Bill	Amount	Jan	Feb	Mar	Apr	May	Jun	Jul	Aug	Sep	Oct	Nov	Dec
			☐	☐	☐	☐	☐	☐	☐	☐	☐	☐	☐	☐
			☐	☐	☐	☐	☐	☐	☐	☐	☐	☐	☐	☐
			☐	☐	☐	☐	☐	☐	☐	☐	☐	☐	☐	☐
			☐	☐	☐	☐	☐	☐	☐	☐	☐	☐	☐	☐
			☐	☐	☐	☐	☐	☐	☐	☐	☐	☐	☐	☐
			☐	☐	☐	☐	☐	☐	☐	☐	☐	☐	☐	☐
			☐	☐	☐	☐	☐	☐	☐	☐	☐	☐	☐	☐
			☐	☐	☐	☐	☐	☐	☐	☐	☐	☐	☐	☐
			☐	☐	☐	☐	☐	☐	☐	☐	☐	☐	☐	☐
			☐	☐	☐	☐	☐	☐	☐	☐	☐	☐	☐	☐
			☐	☐	☐	☐	☐	☐	☐	☐	☐	☐	☐	☐
			☐	☐	☐	☐	☐	☐	☐	☐	☐	☐	☐	☐
			☐	☐	☐	☐	☐	☐	☐	☐	☐	☐	☐	☐
			☐	☐	☐	☐	☐	☐	☐	☐	☐	☐	☐	☐

Monthly Income: Extra Income: Total Income: Total Paid Out: Cash Available:

Food	Gadgets	Other Expenses

Insurance	Payment	Date Paid

Utilities	Payment	Date Paid
Electricity		
Water		
Sanitation		
Phone service		
Internet service		
Cable TV		
Gas		
Total =		

Date	Bill	Amount	Jan	Feb	Mar	Apr	May	Jun	Jul	Aug	Sep	Oct	Nov	Dec

Monthly Income: Extra Income: Total Income: Total Paid Out: Cash Available: